EARTH'S INSECTS
NEED YOU!

Lacewing

by Ruth Owen

With thanks to
Paul Hetherington
Director of Fundraising and Communications
Buglife, UK

Ruby Tuesday Books

Published in 2024 by Ruby Tuesday Books Ltd.

Editor: Mark J. Sachner
Design & Production: Tammy West

Photo credits:
Alamy: 12 (Biosphoto), 27TL (Matthew Taylor); Susie Moon: 29B; Nature Picture Library: 8C (Edwin Giesbers), 8B (Chris Gomershall/2020VISION), 9B (Kim Taylor), 13C (Andy Sands), 13B (Nick Upton), 15B (Mark Moffett), 16B (Suzi Eszterhas), 17TR (Nature Production), 23B (Mark Carwardine); Public Domain: 7B, 19T, 20B; Science Photo Library: 11T (Laguna Design); Shutterstock: Cover TL (2shrimpS), Cover TC (Pop-Thailand), Cover TR (Susan B Sheldon), Cover BL (Minko Peev), Cover CR (mehmetkrc), Cover BR (Olivier Le Queinec), 1 (Wirestock Creators), 4T (Protasov AN), 4B (aabeele), 5T (Harmony Video Production), 5B (Jolanda Aalbers), 6T (Dragon Claws), 6B (Somyot Mali-ngam), 7T (Sam Bateman), 9T (Butterfly Hunter), 9C (Isabelle Ohara), 10L (various), 10R (Nabeel Zaidi), 11CL (Sebastian Photography), 11CR (Jan Pelcman), 11BL (Denis Nata), 11BR (Ramlan Bin Abdul Jalil), 13T (Todorean-Gabriel), 14 (Cosmin Vatris), 15TL (Michael Rads), 15TR (Jan Mastnik), 15CL (Krisana Antharith), 15CR (Young Swee Ming), 16CL (Webb Photography), 16CR (Leena Robinson), 17TL (Leena Robinson), 17C (Darkdiamond67), 17C (Butterfly Hunter), 18T (Rich Carey), 18B (Ewelina W), 19B (Ryzhkov Oleksandr), 20T (Stockr), 21 (Kuttelvaserova Stuchelova), 21BR (Robert Lessman), 22T (Jonas Vegele), 22B (Africa Studio), 23T (A. S. Floro), 24—25 (Golden Shrimp), 24C (Simic Vojislav), 24C (Rawpixel.com), 26T (Dini Liefferink-Medendrop), 26C (Colin Burdett), 27C (L. Feddes), 27B (josefkubes), 27B (Soho A Studio), 27R (various), 28 (ibnu alias), 28 (Keith Hider), 28 (grafvision), 28 (Alexander Raths), 29 (xpixel), 29 (sylv1rob1), 29R (various), 30T (Leslie Brienza), 30T (Fisaga), 30B (T. Photo), 31 (P J Photography), 31 (WorldStockStudio), 31 (Ana Sha), 31 (mehmetkrc); Superstock: 25T (Fitch, Charles Marden).

Library of Congress Control Number: 2023903519

Print (Hardback) ISBN 978-1-78856-283-6
Print (Paperback) ISBN 978-1-78856-284-3
ePub ISBN 978-1-78856-286-7
Published in Minneapolis, MN
Printed in the United States

www.rubytuesdaybooks.com

Contents

Life's Little Essentials

Long before there were humans, other mammals, birds, fish, and even the dinosaurs, there were insects on Earth. From day to day, most people don't notice or even think about them. But insects are all around us, making life on our planet possible.

For every 1 human on Earth, there are 1,400,000,000 insects!

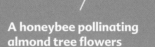

A honeybee pollinating almond tree flowers

Insects are pollinators that help farmers grow many of the fruits, vegetables, and other crops that we eat.

Essential for Survival?

If humans were to become extinct tomorrow, the rest of the natural world would carry on without us. But if insects were to disappear, life on our planet would be impossible.

European bee-eater

Dragonfly

Insects are food for other animals and are an essential part of many food chains.

Fly

Dead mouse

The Decomposers

Flies buzzing around the carcass of a dead animal or a heap of dung may seem disgusting. But the flies will lay eggs, and when their larvae, or maggots, hatch from the eggs, the young insects will feed on the waste material. Without the work of decomposers such as maggots, beetles, ants, and other insects, our world would be a smelly, dangerous mess of rotting bodies, dead plants, and poop.

Predatory insects feed on other insect species, such as aphids, that can destroy trees and crops.

Aphid

Ladybug

But insects are in trouble, and humans are to blame. The destruction of insect-friendly habitats and the use of pesticides are just two of the reasons why insect numbers are falling. However, it's not too late to create a world that is once again a safe and welcoming place for these tiny animals.

It's a big challenge. Are you ready? Because...
... EARTH'S INSECTS NEED YOU!

Their Planet First!

About 90% of the animal species on Earth are insects. They have lived on our planet for around 400 million years and were flying through Earth's skies long before there were pterosaurs or the first birds.

Some insects, such as ants, termites, and bees, evolved to live in huge colonies. The colony is led by a queen who lays eggs and is the mother of all the colony's members.

Within the colony's nest, each tiny insect has a job to do. The thousands, or sometimes millions, of insects in the group survive by working and acting almost as if they are one living thing.

It's All About Teamwork

Weaver ants live in colonies with up to 500,000 members. These ants build their nests from leaves. Worker ants pull together the edges of leaves. Then larvae (baby ants) are carried to the leaf edges. The larvae produce silk from their heads that is used to stitch the leaf edges together.

Weaver ant nest

Worker ant

Larva

Silk

Building for Survival

A termite colony lives in an underground nest. Above ground, worker termites build a mound made of chewed-up plants and billions of tiny mouthfuls of mud. The mound contains chambers and passages and acts like a giant set of lungs. As air flows through the mound, the oxygen needed by the termites for breathing is sucked in and unwanted carbon dioxide is pushed out.

Queen termite

A termite queen can lay 30,000 eggs each day!

Arctic woolly bear caterpillar

Termite mound

Ultimate Survivors

A woolly bear caterpillar spends the Arctic winter asleep and frozen solid! Special chemicals in its body allow it to freeze but not die. In spring, the caterpillar defrosts and starts feeding. It eats for about three weeks and then goes back to sleep. It does this every spring for about 14 years until it is ready to change into a moth.

Insects have lived through ice ages and times when Earth was much hotter than it is today. They survived extinction events, such as comet and asteroid strikes, that wiped out the dinosaurs and other animal groups.

Nothing could destroy the insects.

Until now. UNTIL HUMANS.

Counting Down to a Crisis

Scientists estimate that about 75% of Earth's insects have been lost in the last 50 years. How do we know?

Unlike endangered giant pandas or gorillas, there are no large organizations counting and protecting insects. The data we have about the loss of Earth's insects comes from the hard work of just a small number of entomologists (insect scientists) and volunteers who study insects as their hobby.

In habitats such as forests, meadows, and nature reserves around the world, scientists use traps and nets to capture and count insects. They carry out their insect counts each year in the same area and during the same month.

The Splatter Test

Ask your grandparents about traveling in a car in summer when they were children. The windshield would be splattered with dead insects. Today, this doesn't happen.

The "Bugs Matter" citizen science activity asks people in the UK (United Kingdom) to count insect splats on their car license plates during summer. This splat count shows a 60% drop in insects in the past 20 years.

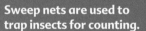
Sweep nets are used to trap insects for counting.

Insects land on this tent-like trap and then fly up into the container.

Butterflies are sometimes counted by people known as recorders. Every two weeks throughout the spring and summer, a recorder walks along a particular route. They count and record the butterflies they see within 6 feet (2 m) of their route.

Gone Forever!

Scientists think there may be 10 million species of insects. However, only about 1 million have been named and studied. Every day, huge areas of the Amazon rain forest and tropical forests in Africa and Asia are destroyed. No one can say how many insects are being lost. Many species may have already become extinct before we ever knew they existed!

Monarch butterfly

The Great Monarch Count

In the United States, large numbers of monarch butterflies spend the winter roosting in trees in California. Each November, more than 100 volunteers visit almost 300 places to count the butterflies. In 2022, the volunteers counted 335,479 butterflies. This number was thankfully an increase from recent years. However, in the 1980s and 1990s, the volunteers would count millions of monarchs each November.

Monarch butterflies roosting in a tree

A Problem Shared

The loss of insects is badly affecting their predators. Spotted flycatchers are small birds who feed on butterflies, moths, craneflies, and damselflies. The numbers of these birds have dropped by 89% since the 1960s! Lack of food is almost certainly one of the reasons that the birds are in trouble.

A spotted flycatcher grabbing a tortoiseshell butterfly in mid flight

Year by year, counts and other studies show that insect numbers are dropping—FAST!

Why Do We Need Insects?
THE POLLINATORS

Some of the foods we eat, such as wheat, oats, and rice, are pollinated by the wind. But many foods we must eat to get essential vitamins and minerals come from plants that need insects to pollinate them before they can produce fruits and vegetables.

Insects help pollinate the plants that produce these foods and drinks.

Bees, butterflies, and moths are well-known pollinators. But have you ever noticed a tiny insect hovering in one place and then darting up, down, or sideways at high speed? These tiny flies are hoverflies, and they can hover in mid-air, beating their wings up to 250 times per second.

Hoverflies soak up nectar from flowers with their sponge-like mouthparts. As they hover and feed, these tiny flies carry pollen from plant to plant.

Hoverfly

Farmers are already struggling to grow some food crops as the numbers of insect pollinators fall.

with their tongues.

Dandelion

Ground squirrel

Save Our Wildflowers!

Wildflowers make our world more beautiful. But the flowers, seeds, and other parts of these plants are also an important food for many animals. Without insect pollinators, 8 out of 10 wildflower plants would die out.

Wildflowers

No Chocolate Without Midges

Chocolate is made from the beans (or seeds) of the cacao tree. The flowers of this tree are so small that only tiny flies called midges can climb inside and move pollen from one flower to another. Without these miniature flies—which are less than one-tenth of an inch (3 mm) long—we would have no chocolate!

Adult fingernail

Cacao tree flower

The Most Important Pollinators

Bees have been on Earth for more than 100 million years. Around the world, there are more than 20,000 species. Bees are divided into three groups—honeybees, bumblebees, and solitary bees.

Honeybees live in colonies of up to 80,000 members. They naturally build hives inside holes in tree trunks and branches.

Fat and furry bumblebees live in colonies with a queen and up to 400 members. Some species build nests under the ground or in compost heaps, while others nest in trees. Solitary bees live alone, and each female builds her own nest.

It's All About the Buzzzzzzzz

The flowers of some plants, such as tomato and pepper plants, must be vibrated so that the anthers (or male parts) release their pollen. A bumblebee visits the anthers of a tomato plant and vibrates her body, which shakes loose the pollen onto her body. This is called buzz pollination.

Anthers

Tomato plant

A bumblebee buzz pollinating

Pollen

A bumblebee uses her legs to comb the pollen from her fur into her pollen baskets. Then she takes the pollen back to her nest. However, some pollen grains remain stuck to her fuzzy body and get carried to the next flower.

Pollen basket

A New Home-Honeybee Style!

When a honeybee colony grows too large, the queen and half the colony leave the hive. Inside the old nest, a new, young queen becomes the old hive's leader. The honeybees swarm (fly around) until they find a place to wait, often hanging in a tree, surrounding their queen.

Next, up to 100 scout bees leave the swarm to search for a new place to live. The scouts look for tree holes that may be the size of the inside of a washing machine or even larger.

Once a scout finds a nest site, she returns to the swarm. She buzzes her wings, wiggles her body, and walks around in a particular pattern. This is called a waggle dance. Each scout's dance tells the swarm about the possible new home they've found.

Eventually, a decision is made, and the honeybees take flight to their new home.

A honeybee swarm

Leafcutter bee

Leafcutter Bees

Leafcutter bees are solitary bees. Females like to nest in small, narrow spaces. A leafcutter bee cuts pieces of leaf from plants. Then she uses them to make tube-like cells inside her nest. Inside each cell she lays an egg. She also puts pollen inside the cell as food for each larva as it hatches.

All types of bees visit flowers to eat and collect nectar and pollen. As they do this, they carry pollen on their bodies from flower to flower. Bees are Earth's most important pollinators of both wild plants and human food crops. And they do all this without realizing how essential their work is to life on Earth.

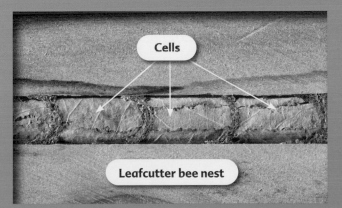

Cells

Leafcutter bee nest

THE CLEAN-UP CREWS

A cow can produce up to 12 cow pies a day, or around 79 pounds (36 kg) of dung! Without insect clean-up crews, farmers' fields would soon be covered by dung and there would be nowhere for animals to graze on grass.

Yellow dung flies mate and lay their eggs on the dung of sheep, cows, and horses. When larvae hatch from the eggs, they live in the dung and feed on it. Dung beetles also quickly arrive at a heap of fresh animal dung. They eat the solid waste and drink any soupy liquid poop.

Yellow dung flies

Dung

Adult yellow dung flies feed on other flies, such as hoverflies.

Along with fungi and bacteria, insects do the vital work of breaking down and cleaning up rotting plants, dung, and dead bodies.

The Dung Rollers

The lives of roller dung beetles start inside a ball of dung. A male and female roller dung beetle meet at a dung pile. Together, they roll the dung to make balls that they bury underground. After mating, the female beetle lays her eggs in the dung balls. When larvae hatch from the eggs, they have a ready-made meal of dung waiting for them.

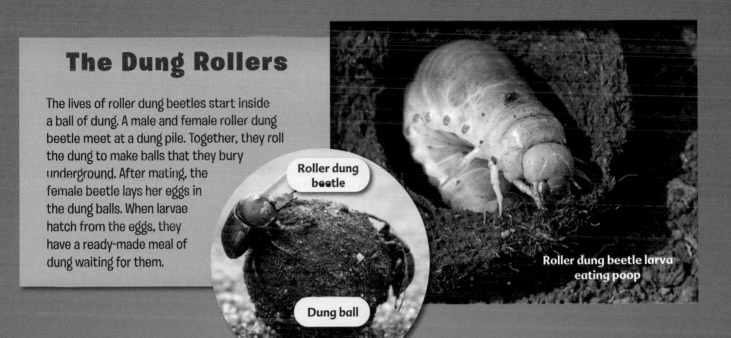

Roller dung beetle

Dung ball

Roller dung beetle larva eating poop

Feeding on Flesh

Dead mouse

Maggots

Bluebottle fly

When it's time for a female bluebottle fly to lay her eggs, she goes in search of the perfect home for her young—a fresh corpse! A single bluebottle can lay more than 500 eggs on a dead body. In less than 48 hours, hundreds of tiny larvae, or maggots, hatch from the eggs. The young flies immediately start feeding on the juicy, rotting flesh.

Burying Food for Baby

When a small animal dies, burying beetles can detect chemicals being released from the body up to 5 miles (8 km) away. If several beetle pairs arrive at the same dead body, they fight—male against male and female against female. The biggest pair usually wins.

The winning pair strips the fur or feathers from the corpse and buries it in soil. Then the beetles mate and the female lays up to 30 eggs close to the meat. When larvae hatch from the eggs, the mother beetle feeds on the rotting meat and regurgitates a meaty soup into the mouths of her young.

Mother burying beetle

Larva

Rotting meat

Why Do We Need Insects?
BECAUSE THEY ARE MIND-BOGGLING-LY AWESOME!

We are so lucky to live alongside tiny animals that make life on our planet possible. But they aren't just useful. They should also fill us with wonder!

One of the most incredible events in the insect world is metamorphosis. This is the almost magical set of changes that insects go through during their life cycle.

1

Monarch butterfly caterpillar

When a butterfly caterpillar hatches from its egg, it immediately starts feeding on the plants that were specially chosen by its mother to be its first home and food supply.

2

Eventually, a great day comes. The caterpillar splits out of its old skin. Underneath is a new, smooth skin but no legs, antennae, or even eyes. Now the insect has entered the pupa stage of its life cycle.

Old caterpillar skin

Mind-Boggling Life Cycles

A sloth moth lives high in a rain forest tree in the fur of a three-toed sloth. When the sloth climbs down to the ground for its weekly poop, a female moth will fly from the sloth's fur and lay her eggs in its dung. When the caterpillars hatch, they live in the dung and eat it, too. Once a caterpillar transforms into an adult moth, it flies up into the treetops to find its own three-toed sloth home.

Adult sloth fur

Baby sloth

Sloth moths

3 Inside its pupal skin or case, many parts of the insect's body dissolve into a soup-like mass of cells. Weeks or months pass by. The cells form new organs and body parts, including a head, thorax, abdomen, and two pairs of colorful wings.

Monarch butterfly pupa

4 Once its transformation is complete, the insect's pupal skin splits open. The new butterfly pumps blood through the veins in its wings so they can open and harden. Finally, the butterfly takes flight, ready to find a mate so that the cycle of life can continue.

Mind-Boggling Survival Tactics

Honeypot ants live in hot, dry deserts. When plants are in bloom, the worker ants collect large quantities of nectar. Then, in the colony's underground nest, they feed the nectar to special workers called repletes. The abdomens of the repletes grow bigger and bigger. Then, during times when there is no food around, the repletes regurgitate the nectar for the whole colony to eat.

Replete worker ant

The ants' abdomens can grow as big as a grape!

Abdomen

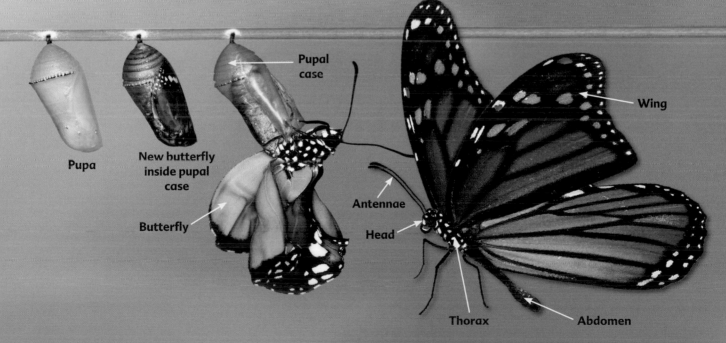

Pupa

New butterfly inside pupal case

Butterfly

Pupal case

Wing

Antennae

Head

Thorax

Abdomen

A butterfly's metamorphosis is every bit as amazing as any plot from a superhero movie. Except in the world of insects, the incredible change from a larva to an adult is. . .

. . . science, not fiction!

What Have We Done?
HABITAT DESTRUCTION

The ways in which humans destroy wild habitats are killing insects and other wild animals all over the world.

When we think of habitat destruction, we might picture a tropical rain forest with large mammals such as orangutans or tigers losing their homes. And we'd be right. Tropical rain forests are burned, bulldozed, or plowed to make space for growing crops.

Tropical rain forest in Malaysia being cleared to grow a crop of palm oil

Forests once **covered 31%** of the land on Earth. Today, only 15% remains.

Who Were Today's 100?

Scientists estimate that every day more than 100 species of plants and animals become extinct in tropical forests.

The front yard of this house has no habitat for wildlife.

But habitat destruction is also happening all around us in small but devastating ways. For example, every time someone removes plants from outside their house to create a concrete-covered parking space, insects lose their home.

Wild meadows, old woodlands, heathland, and wetlands are destroyed to create more farmland or to build highways, housing or industrial developments, shopping centers, and golf courses.

Saving The Happy Man Tree

A tree in London, nicknamed The Happy Man Tree, was at the center of a battle between builders and local people. The builders planned to cut down the tree to make space for new homes. Local campaigners wanted the builders to make the old, but still healthy, tree part of the new housing development. Sadly, in 2021, the 150-year-old tree was cut down!

A huge wheat field

As wild places disappear, insects become trapped in shrinking patches of habitat...

...that just get
...smaller... and smaller.

Changing Farmland

If you'd visited a British farm 100 years ago, you would have seen small fields filled with lots of different crops. Grasses for making hay would share the soil with nettles, poppies, and other wildflowers. Fields were separated by hedgerows of blackberry bushes and other plants and small trees.

But after World War II, the government wanted more food production. Between 1950 and 2000, about 6,000 miles (9,600 km) of hedgerows were destroyed each year. The countryside changed to vast fields, often growing just one kind of crop.

The land could now produce more food for people. But the mixture of crops, hedgerows, wildflowers, and weeds was gone. So was the perfect habitat for insects, birds, and other wildlife.

What Have We Done?
PESTICIDES

When humans grow crops, living things known as "pests" can eat or attack them. To protect their plants, farmers use chemicals called pesticides to kill insects, rats, weeds, or fungi. The chemicals designed for killing insects are known as insecticides.

Nowhere Is Safe!

Many types of insecticides are sprayed onto crops. The poisons can be carried by the wind far from a farm's fields. They can even be blown into protected nature reserves that are meant to be safe places for wildlife.

Spraying fields with chemicals

A crop on a farm may be treated up to **16 times** in a year with different poisonous chemicals!

CROSS COUNTRY

insect spray

CONTAINING 50% DDT
RE: PATENT NO. 22,922

destroys many common insects

USE ON POTATOES, PEAS, CORN, FRUITS and ORNAMENTALS

No. 1365

NET CONTENTS 1 LB.

A DDT container from the 1960s

In the late 1930s, an insecticide called DDT was created. DDT didn't only kill the aphids, caterpillars, and other plant-eating insects that were feeding on crops. It could kill any insect it touched, and it also poisoned birds. By 2004, DDT was banned worldwide. But even today, leftover traces of this chemical can still be found in soil and rivers!

In the late 1990s, hundreds of thousands of honeybees that were feeding on sunflower crops began to die. Scientists discovered that chemicals called neonicotinoids were to blame. The poisons were designed to kill plant-eating insects such as caterpillars, weevils, and beetles. But the poison had spread to the flowers' pollen and to nectar that was collected by the bees.

In 2018, neonicotinoids were banned in the UK and countries in the EU (European Union). But farmers can still get special permission from their government to use these poisons if there is an outbreak of pests and farmers believe it is an emergency.

Killer Neonicotinoids

One of the ways that neonicotinoids are used is on seeds. A seed is coated with the chemical. Once the seed is in the ground, the chemical dissolves and is taken up by the plant's roots along with water. This means that the poison spreads to every part of the plant—including its pollen and nectar.

When scientists tested wildflowers growing near crops treated with neonicotinoids, these plants also contained the chemicals. The poisons had spread through the soil in rainwater.

Neonicotinoids affected honeybees in many ways. Queen bees that fed on poisoned nectar laid fewer eggs. Worker bees became confused and could not find food or find their way back to their hives.

Honeybees

A dead honeybee

The production of pesticides is a huge, money-making industry. So, when one chemical is banned, another one soon takes its place.

What Have We Done?
UNDER ATTACK!

Habitat destruction and pesticides are not the only dangers facing insects.

Garden tiger moth caterpillar

Weeds or Wildflowers?

In a field, wild plants, or weeds, may compete for water and food with a farmer's crops. To protect the crops, farmers kill the weeds with chemicals called herbicides. Counties and towns often spray herbicides at the sides of roads and on pavements to kill weeds. And people use weed killers in their gardens. The problem is that herbicides kill insects and the weeds that they feed on.

Garden tiger moth caterpillars eat dandelions and other wild plants. The numbers of this moth have dropped by 90% in the last 50 years.

Feeding Plants, Killing Insects

Farmers use chemicals called fertilizers to feed their plants with extra nutrients. But some of these chemicals are toxic to insects. For example, when caterpillars feed on the leaves of plants that contain chemical fertilizers, they can be poisoned. This means fewer butterflies and moths.

Good Guys or Bad Guys?

Why are people excited to see a beautiful butterfly in their garden, but will then call her caterpillars "pests" and buy toxic chemicals to kill them? If a robin or sparrow flew into your home, would you pick up a can of "KILL THAT BIRD" and blast the bird until it lay dead on the floor? If not, why is it OK to do this to an insect when all it is doing is looking for food or checking out its environment?

KILL THAT BIRD

Beware Invaders

In a natural habitat, the insects and other animals live together and feed on each other without problems. There is a natural balance. Animals may also have evolved to live with the diseases and pests in their area. But humans have taken many animals to places where they don't belong.

- Asian hornets came to Europe, probably in goods being transported from China. These predatory insects are now hunting European bees.

Asian hornet

- Asian honeybees became infected with tiny parasites called varroa mites, which kill bees. When people moved Asian honeybee colonies around the world, the mites went too and spread to honeybees worldwide.
- Rats arrived in New Zealand aboard ships. The rats ate many local animals, including large, flightless crickets called giant wetas. These insects are now nearly extinct.

Numbered blue chip for monitoring the insect

This giant weta was bred in a zoo and is being released into a forest.

Dangers from Insects

Some insects can, of course, be harmful to humans. Mosquitoes are tiny, biting flies. Some species carry diseases such as malaria and zika virus. Warming temperatures due to climate change may cause the numbers of these insects to increase. They may also spread to live in more countries.

Earth's Changing Climate

Earth's climate is warming up, and this could create great problems for insects.

- Floods, forest fires, and hurricanes caused by climate change will kill insects and destroy their nests. Droughts may kill the plants that insects feed on.
- Over time, insects that need cool habitats may try to move away from hotter areas. But they will only survive if their new homes have the right habitat and foods.
- Bumblebee queens hibernate until early spring. When they wake up, they urgently need to feed on nectar. But warmer days may cause some spring flowers to appear early. By the time the bees are awake, the flowers might have died!

Insects have every right to live safely on Earth. And humans also need them to be able to grow food and survive.

So, what can we do?

What Can We Do to Help?

The good news is that it's not too late to save Earth's insects.

Farms cover about 40% of the land on Earth. If more farms become wildlife-friendly, it will be a great start. It may seem that farmers need to use insecticides and herbicides to grow enough food for everyone on Earth. But every year, about one-third of the food that's grown worldwide is thrown away or left to rot in fields. And in some parts of the world, people are eating far more food than they actually need!

Many scientists, farmers, and conservationists think we could grow all the food we need *AND* be kind to nature. People could still afford to buy this food, and farmers and stores would still make money.

A farmer's market

Calling All Governments

- Governments could give more money, called subsidies, to help people set up organic farms that help nature. These farms would be chemical-free and have habitat for wildlife, such as trees and hedgerows.

- Every government could set a target for how many organic farms its area should have in 10 years, 20 years, and so on. And local neighborhood groups could set up more markets where organic or local farmers could sell their food.

- Very few insects are protected by law. A government can change this. An insect is as important as an eagle or whale. These laws could stop people destroying the habitat of a protected insect.

- Governments could add high taxes to insecticides, herbicides, and chemical fertilizers to make them more expensive to use.

Stag beetles in the UK are endangered and need more protection.

A Bug Baby Boom

Most insects are very good at reproducing. A queen honeybee can lay 2,000 eggs each day. And every egg can become a new worker bee in just 20 days. If we give them the chance, insects will rebuild their numbers—fast!

Dig for an Insect Victory!

During World War II, people were asked to grow food and "Dig for Victory." Today, billions of dollars are spent each year around the world on medical care and projects to help people who are not eating healthily. What if some of this money was used to set up community gardens in every village, town, and city where people could grow their own fruit and vegetables? Governments could even send people free seeds! Gardening would be good for people's bodies and their mental health. And these spaces would be the perfect habitat for insects.

Sphinx moth caterpillar

Wasp larvae feeding on the caterpillar

Community gardens on the edge of a town

Nature's Got This!

If farmers don't use pesticides, won't insects destroy their crops? The truth is that most insects that are seen as pests already have their own natural predators. Aphids are the food of hoverflies, ladybugs, beetles, lacewings, and birds. Some types of wasps capture caterpillars and take them back to their nests to feed to their larvae. Other wasps inject their eggs into caterpillars. When the wasp larvae hatch, they feed on the caterpillar from the inside out.

A Better World for Everyone

Local and county governments can put laws in place to make sure that villages, towns, and cities are friendly to insects.

Rules could say that when new buildings, such as homes or factories, are constructed, there must always be a place for wildlife. This might include creating gardens, green roofs, or walls, planting fruit trees that produce blossom, and making ponds for aquatic insects.

An emperor dragonfly laying her eggs in a park pond

Wildflowers growing in a cemetery

Many local governments and neighborhood groups are already doing a great job creating wild areas in parks. They are also planting wildflowers along the sides of roads, at street crossings, and in cemeteries. Governments should ban the use of pesticides by gardeners and neighborhood groups.

Insects Go to School

Governments could work with schools to make sure there was time each week to learn about trees, pollination, soil, and food production. And every school should have a garden where the students can make compost, grow fruits and vegetables, and maybe even care for a small pond!

When wild places are created for insects, it also helps spiders, snails, worms, birds, frogs, toads, and every other animal in an area—big or small! The scent of flowers, the buzzing of bees, and the singing of birds will also make the world a more beautiful and calming place for us busy humans.

26

Planting B-Lines

A UK charity called Buglife has started an exciting project called B-Lines. Just like stepping stones for insects, B-Lines will create thousands of patches of insect habitat that all join up across the UK. This project will allow insects to spread out and find new homes, sources of food, and mates. Everyone in the UK can take part by creating their own stepping stone and adding it to an online map.

A bee might travel from a wildflower meadow near a factory or business park ...

... to a tiny city garden...

... to a green roof on a school...

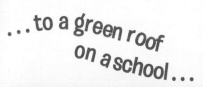

...to a flowerpot on a doorstep...

...and onward!

If We Lose Some Insects, Does It Matter?

Yes! Because all habitats need biodiversity, which is a mixture of different living things that form food chains and food webs. If some insects are lost from a habitat, the animals that rely on them for food will also be in danger.

Falcon

⬆

Starling

⬆

Wasp

⬆

Caterpillar

⬆

Plants

Insects are part of almost all food chains on land.

Get Your Hands Dirty!

Schoolwork, exams, jobs, paying the bills—we all have loads to think about. But there are lots of small actions we can fit into our busy lives to help insects.

NO to Plastic Grass!

Is your family thinking of switching from real grass to plastic? Please say NO! Plastic grass smothers the ground underneath and prevents tiny animals from living in the soil. It's also useless as a habitat or food source for insects. Offer to do the mowing to protect this important habitat. (And leave some areas long so wildflowers can grow!)

Be a Bee Spy

What flowers does a bee visit? You may be surprised to see that it ignores the expensive, colorful plant from a garden center and feeds from the little clover flowers or dandelions growing in the lawn. Notice which plants pollinators like best, and let these grow.

Clover

Cuckoo bee

Ask the adults who take care of you if you can join a local wildlife protection group. You might get to do a pond clean-up or an insect count or take part in planting wildflowers on an unwanted piece of ground near your home.

Grow for You AND Them

All you need to grow tomatoes is a tomato plant from a garden center, some compost, and a large flowerpot or bucket. (You can check out how to do it online.) A plant that costs just a few dollars might produce 200 tomatoes! No plastic packaging. No food miles. And your plant's flowers will be a source of food for bumblebees.

Got a few pieces of untreated old wood? Ask if these can be left in the corner of your garden or yard. They will become a habitat for insects and other small animals such as woodlice.

Home to Rent

Ask for an insect hotel for a birthday or holiday present. The pieces of bamboo cane are a perfect habitat for a leafcutter bee's nest.

Bamboo cane

Pond in an Hour!

A dishpan, some pebbles, and water can become a habitat for tiny water insects and a place where bees, wasps, and other small animals can drink.

Escape route for any insect that can't swim

A Menu for Pollinators

A small corner of a garden or yard, a window box, or even a flowerpot on a doorstep or balcony can be a habitat for insects. Here are some plants you can grow from seed that are favorites with pollinators.

Sunflowers   **Cosmos**   **Rosemary**

Yarrow   **Pea plants**   **Cranesbill**

Nasturtiums   **Foxgloves**   **Oregano**

Thyme   **Lavender**   **Viper's bugloss**

Leek and onion plants   **Poppies**   **Borage**

Make Your Voice Count!

Be a Savvy Consumer

Ask if you can visit a farmers' market and buy some locally grown fruit and vegetables. Ask the farmers what they do to protect insects. If they can't tell you, thank them, but walk away and try another grower. REMEMBER! Customers have power and farmers and shops take notice.

Email your local government, neighborhood group, or representative of your area. Ask them to stop using pesticides in parks, on pavements, and at the sides of roads.

Become a Politician!

Political parties usually have organizations for young people to join. When you are old enough, get involved, and maybe one day you could be making the world a better place as an elected lawmaker in your government!

THERE IS NO PLANET B

Get Ready to Vote

When there's an election, go online and read what the different political parties will do to protect the environment. You may not be able to vote yet. BUT GET READY!

Become a Scientist!

If you love insects, study science at school. One day your job might be researching insects and helping to save them.

If you're asked to do a science project for school, make it about insects and spread the word.

Monster Munchers

Ask your family and friends not to use chemicals in their gardens or yards. Instead, work with nature. Cabbage white butterflies lay their eggs on cabbages, kale, and other green vegetables. Then their caterpillars munch through the vegetables. But the caterpillars will also eat nasturtiums. Plant colorful nasturtiums in your vegetable patch to tempt the insects away from your vegetables.

Cabbage white caterpillar

Don't Lose the Love Bug

Were you fascinated by bugs when you were little? NEVER lose your love for insects. Your play station or social media might seem more important right now. But REMEMBER! These things won't be of much use if insects continue to die and there's nothing left to eat.

Do you have a toddler or young child in your family? Be the one to show them a buzzing bee or a busy ant and turn them into a bug lover.

Pass It On

Tell two people what you've learned from this book. If they both also tell two people, the word will soon spread.

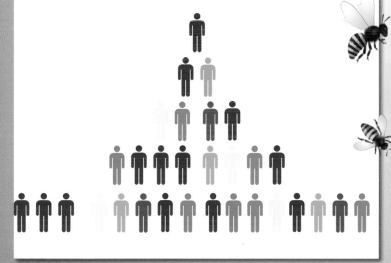

Monarch butterfly

Let's give these tiny animals some LOVE!

Never forget that insects are wonderful, fascinating animals—just like elephants, sharks, eagles, or even your pets.

The future of Earth's insects is in all our hands.

Glossary

biodiversity
The variety and mixture of living things on Earth or in a particular habitat.

conservationist
A person who does work to protect plants, animals, and natural habitats.

data
Facts and numbers that have been collected in order for people to study them.

decomposer
A living thing, such as an insect, bacteria, or fungi, that breaks down matter, such as dead plants, dead bodies, or dung.

evolve
To change little by little over a long time.

metamorphosis
A big change. In insects, it's the process of changing from a larva to an adult.

organic
In farming, growing or producing food without using human-made chemicals and without harming wildlife and natural habitats.

pesticide
A substance (usually made from chemicals) that is used to kill insects, rodents, weeds, fungi, bacteria, or other pests.

pollinator
An insect or other animal that carries pollen from flower to flower. Many flowering plants need animals to do this so that they can make seeds.

species
Different types of living things. The members of an animal species can produce young together.

weed
A wild plant. People may call it a weed because it is growing where it is not wanted.

Index